CATERPILLAR MILITARY TRACTORS

TRACTORS

VOLUME 1 PHOTO ARCHIVE

CATERPILLAR MILITARY TRACTORS

VOLUME 1 PHOTO ARCHIVE

Photographs from the
Caterpillar Inc. Corporate Archives

Edited with introduction by
P. A. Letourneau

Iconografix
Photo Archive Series

Iconografix
P.O. Box 18433
Minneapolis, Minnesota 55418 USA

Library of Congress Card Number 94-76266

ISBN 1-882256-16-6

94 95 96 97 98 99 00 5 4 3 2 1

Cover and book design by Lou Gordon, Osceola, Wisconsin

Printed in the United States of America

Book trade distribution by Voyageur Press, Inc. (800) 888-9653

PREFACE

The histories of machines and mechanical gadgets are contained in the books, journals, correspondence and personal papers stored in libraries and archives throughout the world. Written in tens of languages, covering thousands of subjects, the stories are recorded in millions of words.

Words are powerful. Yet, the impact of a single image, a photograph or an illustration, often relates more than dozens of pages of text. Fortunately, many of the libraries and archives that house the words also preserve the images.

In the *Photo Archive Series*, Iconografix reproduces photographs and illustrations selected from public and private collections. The images are chosen to tell a story—to capture the character of their subject. Reproduced as found, they are accompanied by the captions made available by the archive.

The Iconografix *Photo Archive Series* is dedicated to young and old alike, the enthusiast, the collector and anyone who, like us, is fascinated by "things" mechanical.

ACKNOWLEDGMENTS

The photographs, captions, and related information included in this book were made available by the Caterpillar Inc. Corporate Archives. We are grateful to Caterpillar Inc. and to Joyce Luster, Corporate Archivist, for permission to reproduce the materials.

Peoria on the Ledo Road, the Bingham painting that illustrated Caterpillar advertisements of November 1944.

INTRODUCTION

Since the early years of World War I, Caterpillar tractors, engines, and power units have played critical roles in military campaigns around the globe. The first Caterpillar tractors to enter military service were sold by the Holt Manufacturing Company to the French War Department in 1914. Sales to the British and Russian governments followed in 1915. The Ordinance Division of the United States Army ordered its first Caterpillars in 1916. The tractors were used to move artillery and to transport ammunition and other supplies, previously the work of horses. Wartime demand for Caterpillars was such that the Holt factories were operated six days a week. By the end of World War I, the Stockton and Peoria plants had produced 5,082 tractors for the various military. Another 4,689 tractors were built by other manufacturers under Holt patent license and with the company's supervision.

Sales to the military diminished during the 1920s and 30s. The onset of World War II, however, brought a renewed demand. In 1940, 30 percent of Caterpillar Tractor Company's production was shipped overseas for use in military construction. The United States' entry into the war escalated the demand for bulldozers, road graders, engines, and electric sets to the point that 85 percent of the company's output went directly to the government. Military sales during the Korean War were significant as well, and Caterpillar equipment played a vital role in support of the United Nations' actions.

Caterpillar Military Tractors Photo Archive, Volume 1 and *Volume 2* feature photographs of the Caterpillar machines that saw action in the United States' invasion of Mexico in 1916, World War I, World War II, and the Korean War. While many of the tractors were photographed on the battlefield or behind Allied lines, most were either photographed at the factory or during field trials carried out by the military. *Volume 1* includes a special section covering World War I-era Caterpillar self-propelled gun mounts. *Volume 2* includes a special section covering the Caterpillar Diesel Military Engine or RD-1820, the air-cooled radial engine developed by the company in 1941 for use in M4 tanks. Both volumes include reproductions of paintings commissioned by Caterpillar and used in the company's advertisements during World War II.

UNITED STATES INVASION OF MEXICO

WORLD WAR I

General Pershing (at left) and his staff observe Caterpillar tractors during Mexican border tests.

Holt 75 with trainload on the Mexican border.

United States Quartermaster Corps (USQMC) Holt 75 with Caterpillar trailers operating near the Mexican border.

USQMC Holt 75 with Caterpillar trailers operating at the Mexican border.

Holt tractors on arrival in England, about 1915. Photo taken along the well-known White Cliffs of Dover.

Holt 18 on display during parade. Peoria 1917.

Camouflaged Holt 120.

Armoured 10 Ton, the Model 55 Artillery Tractor.

Armoured 10 Ton, the Model 55 Artillery Tractor.

Armoured 10 Ton, the Model 55 Artillery Tractor.

Holt 5 Ton at a 3rd Army carnival. Koblenz, Germany. April 1919.

Somewhere in France.

A demonstration of the Model 45 at Fort Sill, Oklahoma. 1915.

Holt 45 Model E HVS with winch and armour.

Pikes Peak hill climb during U.S. Army trials.

Caterpillar tests carried out by the USQMC in 1916.

Model 60 in Salonica, Greece. 1915.

Two Holt 45s and one Holt 75 of the Tractor Section, Camp Joseph E. Johnston, Florida.

Holt 120 during U.S. Army Engineering tests in Leon Springs, Texas. 1917.

Armoured Model 18. 1915.

Armoured Model 18. 1915.

Long Track 120 during 1918 Army tests.

Long Track 45 climbing a steep bank near the Peoria plant during World War I trials. (The Long Track 45 was built mostly from Stockton components. In general, however, Stockton supplied engines while Peoria supplied the remaining components and assembled the tractors.)

Holt 18 on bad roads during government tests.

3rd Field Artillery Brigade Division in Germany.

Armoured 10 Ton.

Armoured 10 Ton.

Caterpillars pulling 42 centimeter howitzers captured from the Germans in Belgium.

Top view of a camouflaged Armoured 5 Ton.

Front view of an Armoured 5 Ton with armoured doors open.

Holt 18 on test at Ft. Sam Houston, Texas. 1917.

Long Track 120 during 1918 tests.

Long Track 120 during 1918 tests.

Holt 120 pulling a Caterpillar Wagon and Holt 10 Ton.

USQMC trials of the 10 Ton.

USQMC trials of the 10 Ton.

A demonstration of the Model 45 at Fort Sill, Oklahoma. 1915.

A 5 Ton in military service in the Northwest Frontier.

U.S. Army 5 Ton and two 5 ton trailers at the factory.

A Holt 75 with Holt 20 ton wagon moving Illinois National Guardsmen from Eckwood Park to Glen Oak Park, Illinois.

U.S. government Stockton-built 75s. 1916.

Testing the climbing characteristics of a Long Track 45. 1917.

A demonstration of the Model 45 at Fort Sill, Oklahoma. 1915.

Camouflaged 10 Ton.

Camouflaged 10 Ton under testing for the U.S. Army.

Holt 18 on test for the U.S. Army. Peoria 1918.

Holt 120 and Caterpillar wagon under testing for the U.S. Army.

Holt 18 procured from Holt for testing. Tractor with 6-inch Howitzer passing through mud hole. November 1917.

Model 45 Artillery Armoured Tractor. Right front view, armoured doors open. May 1919.

Holt 75 on test at Fort Sam Houston, Texas. 1917.

Model 75 drawing a big gun up in position.

An 8-inch howitzer being towed by a Holt 120.

Model 45 hauling a big gun on the Western front.

Model 45 hauling big gun up in position.

Long Track 45 climbing a steep bank near Peoria plant during World War I trials.

Armoured 10 Ton, the Model 55 Artillery Tractor.

A 3rd Army 10 Ton and 155 millimeter gun in Germany.

Armoured 10 Ton at the factory.

Holt 18 on test at Ft. Sam Houston, Texas. 1917.

Holt Twentys and Thirty with artillery.

CATERPILLAR GUN MOUNTS

During World War I, Pliny E. Holt served in the United States Ordinance Department. Working with Major James B. Dillard, Holt developed a self-propelled track-type gun mount for high caliber guns and howitzers. The war ended about the time that the first two prototypes were completed. Thereafter, the government transferred further development and production to the Holt factory in Stockton.

The following account of Caterpillar gun mount construction is extracted from a booklet published by Holt and preserved in the Caterpillar Inc. Corporate Archives.

"CATERPILLAR" GUN MOUNT CONSTRUCTION

Unquestionably the greatest artillery product of the great World War, though it played no active part in the war, was the "Caterpillar" Self-Propelled Gun Mount. It has always been one of the greatest problems of the artillery to keep pace with the infantry in open warfare. In the late war, a nearer approach to the solution of this problem was made than ever before. This was achieved by means of the "Caterpillar" Artillery Tractors, that hauled cannon and ammunition over difficult terrain, that would have been almost impossible by any other means. The "Caterpillar" Tractors enabled the artillery really to take the field, independent of railways and good highways. But their usefulness was limited in some cases by the difficulty of pulling cannon or trailers over ground that the tractors themselves would have no trouble traveling over. This difficulty was overcome in part, but only in part, by equipping cannon and trailers with "Caterpillar" Tracks. Other disadvantages remained, among them the difficulty and delay of maneuvering for placing cannon in difficult positions, and the increasing efficiency of observation methods is constantly increasing the necessity of placing the artillery in well-hidden places of difficult accessibility. It has become apparent, therefore, that the ideal artillery unit is a self-propelled gun mount, and steps toward the design and manufacture of such a vehicle were taken soon after this country's entry into the war.

Mr. Pliny E. Holt, who was closely associated with Benjamin Holt in the invention and perfection of the "Caterpillar" Tractor, and who had for many years been actively engaged in tractor design and development work, was persuaded to sever his connection with The Holt Manufacturing Company and take charge of the "Caterpillar" Gun Mount development work for the government. The Marks I, II, III and IV were designed and constructed during the war and the first machines had completed exhaustive and severe tests and were ready for production at the time the armistice was signed. The cessation of hostilities, of course, halted all production plans, but the four self-propelled mounts produced opened a vast field of such importance and extent that orders were issued for the continuation of the work under Government contract and supervision at the Stockton, California plant of The Holt Manufacturing Company. Marks VI, VII and IX were built at Stockton during 1919, 1920 and 1921.

Summing up the achievements up to the completion of the Mark IX, it has been proved that self-propelled "Caterpillar" Gun Mounts can be produced to carry guns and howitzers of considerable size; that speeds of travel of 12 to 13 miles per hour can be maintained continuously, and speeds as high as 30 miles per hour reached in emergency; that the mounts can negotiate extremely steep grades, soft ground and rough ground; that the motor can be waterproofed to permit travel across streams of such depth that the machine is completely submerged; that the mounts have perfect stability for firing; that the shocks of firing do no harm to the propelling mechanism of the mount.

MARK I GUN MOUNT

The Mark I "Caterpillar" Gun Mount was constructed during the war by the U.S. Ordinance Department under the direction of Mr. Pliny E. Holt. Its total weight is 58,000 pounds, the gun alone—the 8-inch howitzer of the British Mark VIII 1/2 type—weighing 7,728 pounds. This gun fires a 200 pound projectile and has a range of 12,100 yards, maximum elevation of 45 degrees and traverse of 8 degrees. The mount has a gas engine as its power plant and travels at speeds of 1 to 4 miles per hour. The vehicle measures 284 inches in length, 108 inches in height and 118 inches in width.

The same elevation and traverse of the top carriage are possible with this mount as with the standard wheel carriage. It is, of course, easily possible to obtain a traverse of 360 degrees by maneuvering the entire mount.

The main frame of the vehicle is of cast steel of the box section type, with an opening in the center for the recoil of the gun. The location of the gun toward the front of the carriage makes this mount extremely stable.

Two of the Mark I mounts were completed and tested prior to the signing of the armistice, the tests proving entirely satisfactory.

MARK II GUN MOUNT

The Mark II "Caterpillar" Gun Mount carries a 155 mm. gun of the 1918 model. The gun weighs 8,750 pounds; mount and gun complete weigh 61,000 pounds. This gun fires a 95 pound projectile a distance of 17,717 yards. The vehicle is slightly shorter and lower than the Mark I, the over-all dimensions being—length, 284 inches; height, 96 inches; width, 118 inches.

The cast steel main frame of this mount is U-shaped in the rear to leave an opening for the recoil of the gun. This construction makes loading easier than in the case of the howitzer on the Mark I.

The power plant of the Mark II is a gas engine, mounted under the forward end of the gun. The Mark II travels at speeds of 1.3 to 5.4 miles per hour.

In the Mark II, as well as in all of the other early mounts, developed during the war, standard "Caterpillar" Tractor parts were used to the fullest possible extent, in order to expedite development and production and to avoid further demands upon the already heavily burdened munitions industry.

Eight of the Mark II "Caterpillar Gun Mounts were built and have been placed in the hands of the troops.

MARK III GUN MOUNT

The Mark III "Caterpillar" Gun Mount was designed to carry a bigger gun than any of the vehicles developed up to that time—the 240 mm. howitzer, 1918 model, which weighs 10,790 pounds and fires a 356 pound projectile a distance of 1700 yards.

The total weight of the vehicle and gun is 106,300 pounds, a weight that is somewhat objectionable as it is in excess of the weight limit set by U.S. engineers for standard highway bridges. The weight, moreover, seems excessive in view of later developments in gun mount design, which is also true of the Marks I and II. It must be remembered, however, that these first mounts were an emergency development, designed and built in a limited amount of time and with the idea that it might be necessary to start production before much field experience had been accumulated. A very liberal margin of strength of all parts was therefore provided, resulting in great weights.

The Mark III measures 297 1/2 inches in length, 113 inches in height and 118 inches in width. It has road speeds of 1 to 4.3 miles per hour. It is equipped with a specially designed top carriage provided with an auxiliary recoil system. The mount proved so stable, however, as to make this auxiliary recoil unnecessary.

MARK IV GUN MOUNT

The Mark IV "Caterpillar" Gun Mount marks a rather unique departure in the design of these vehicles. While designed as a mount for the same howitzer as the Mark III, this mount consists of two vehicles, both having chassis of practically the same design, and both being driven by electric motors. One vehicle carries the gun, the other carries the gas engine generating plant and also serves as a limber to carry 42 rounds of ammunition. In traveling on the road, the two vehicles are hitched together and a heavy cable carries the electric power from the limber to the gun mount. For crossing bridges or maneuvering in limited areas, it is possible to use a long extension cable that allows the gun mount considerable range of movement semi-independent of the generator.

The gun mount member of this pair of vehicles has the same style of top carriage and the same recoil system as the Mark III. A screw jack form of outrigger adds stability for firing.

The Mark IV avoids the excessive weight of the Mark III, each of the vehicles weighing only 71,500 pounds. The total length is 367 inches, height 156 inches and width 102 inches. The mount has road speeds of 1 to 8 miles.

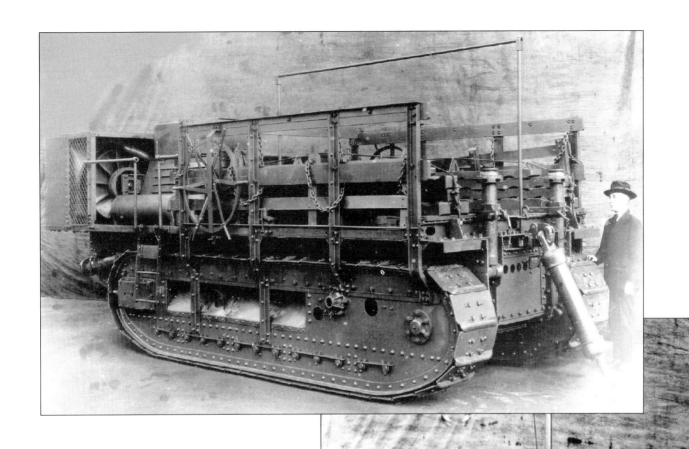

MARK VI GUN MOUNT

The Mark VI "Caterpillar" Gun Mount is shown in this order to preserve the numerical rotation. Actually, however, it was designed and built after the Mark VII and represents many important developments. The Mark VI is, in fact, the high point of achievement up to the present time in the smaller class of mounts. It carries, interchangeably, either the 75 mm. gun or 105 mm. howitzer of the 1920 models. It weighs, complete, only 13,000 pounds. It is waterproofed to permit operation of the propelling mechanism in considerable depths of water—a valuable feature for crossing rivers independent of bridges. Most important of all, it travels at speeds of 1 to 30 miles per hour.

The Mark VI was built at the Stockton plant of The Holt Manufacturing Company during 1920-1921. Departing from the use of standard tractor parts, the motor, track and all other parts were specially designed. A novel departure is the extensive use of rubber in the construction, rubber pads being provided for the track shoes, and rubber rims for the truck wheels, drive sprocket, idler and track carrier rollers. Severe and prolonged tests proved that the rubber withstands a remarkable amount of wear and is of immense value in absorbing shocks and vibration and preventing damage to road surfaces, making possible and practicable the high speeds of travel achieved by this mount.

The Mark VI is equipped with light outriggers and shows perfect stability in firing tests. It is a remarkably quiet-running vehicle. The ground-pressure under the tracks is less than 6 pounds per square inch. The Mark VI is only 77 inches wide, 76 inches high and 160 inches long. It turns in a 104-inch radius.

MARK VII GUN MOUNT

The Mark VII "Caterpillar" Gun Mount was built in Stockton during 1919. It was the first mount constructed for guns of 75 mm. caliber and it was the exhaustive tests of this vehicle that developed the many desirable features and improvements later incorporated in the Mark VI. The Mark VII is largely an assembled job, extensive use being made of parts from the 2 1/2 ton "Caterpillar" Artillery Tractor, and a Cadillac motor being used for the power plant.

The Mark VII weighs 10,600 pounds complete, which includes the 749 pound 75 mm. gun of the model of 1916. The Mark VII is slightly smaller than the Mark VI, its length being 135 inches, height 63 inches and width 71 inches.

The Mark VII was the first mount to employ the waterproofing system and demonstrate the possibility of under-water operation. The Mark VII also developed higher speeds of travel—3 to 15 miles per hour—than had ever before been achieved in any vehicle of the tractor type, and opened the way for the further development along this line that resulted in the 30 miles-per-hour maximum of the Mark VI.

While the Mark VII is now displaced by the Mark VI, the VII is of interest as a necessary and important step in the development of the ideal type of mount for guns of small caliber.

MARK IX GUN MOUNT

The Mark IX "Caterpillar" Gun Mount is the newest and most perfect of the larger size mounts. Like the Mark VI, it is a dual purpose mount, carrying either a 155 mm. gun or an 8 inch howitzer of the 1920 models. The Mark IX weighs complete only 45,000 pounds. It is driven by a 250 horsepower, 6 cylinder gas engine, and will develop road speeds as high as 12 to 16 miles per hour.

The total length of the Mark IX is 287 inches, height 81 inches and width 110 inches.

The Mark IX makes extensive use of rubber for tires of revolving track parts. In consequence, the Mark IX is remarkably quiet-running and able to achieve comparatively high speeds of travel with destructive effect upon the mechanism of the mount.

This mount has floating outriggers to aid stability and waterproofing to permit travel in water up to seven-foot depths.

WORLD WAR II

KOREAN WAR

5th Army Caterpillar D4 crossing the Volturno River in Italy on a pontoon bridge. October 1943.

One More River to Cross, the Lyman Anderson painting that illustrated Caterpillar advertisements of November 1942.

Caterpillar D7 with LeTourneau Carryall scraper hauling sand to fill in soft spots of a section of an airfield somewhere in Alaska.

U.S. Marine Corps Caterpillar D8 towing a civilian car up an almost impassable grade on the Pan-American Highway near Guatemala City, Guatemala. September 1943.

Caterpillar D7 with LeTourneau bulldozer filling in a crater left by a 500 pound bomb dropped in North Africa. January 1943.

Bomber Squadron, the painting that illustrated Caterpillar advertisements of December 1942. Artist unknown.

Caterpillar D8 pulling a scraper operated by a Seabee unit, at work on an unfinished section of the 21st Air Force Base on Tinian in the Marianas. Overhead are three B-29s of the Superfortress Fleet. February 1945.

Untitled. Artist Unknown.

U.S. Forces invading Attu, the most westerly of the Aleutian Islands. Scattered over the beach were soldiers, equipment, and supplies for U.S. troops who had debarked from transports off shore. In the foreground is a Caterpillar Diesel Tractor with Athey track-type trailer hauling material. June 14, 1943.

They Fought the Battle of Pelican Rapids, the Geoffry Biggs painting that illustrated Caterpillar advertisements of July and August 1943.

Caterpillar D4 with LaPlant-Choate bulldozer clearing bomb wreckage from the streets in Naples, Italy. November 1943.

As Fast as Troops Can March, the Clymer painting that illustrated Caterpillar advertisements of August and September 1943.

Untitled. Artist Bingham.

Hooking a 37 millimeter anti-tank gun to a Caterpillar D4 to be pulled to position farther inland. Massacre Bay, Attu, Aleutian Islands. May 1943.

Caterpillar Diesel No. 12 Motor Grader grading roads at Camp San Luis Obispo, California. March 29, 1941.

Untitled. Artist unknown.

What the Little Jap General Forgot, the Geoffrey Biggs painting that illustrated Caterpillar advertisements of March 1943.

Thunder over Africa, the M. de V. Lee painting that illustrated Caterpillar advertisements of March 1943.

Caterpillar D8 with LeTourneau bulldozer pushing over palm trees on an island somewhere in the South Pacific. July 1944.

Caterpillar D8s with bulldozers working on an airstrip at Eniwetok, Marshall Islands. October 1944.

U.S. Army Caterpillar D7 moving a 14° ton gun from one location to another. Fort Kamehamaha, Oahu, Hawaii. October 1940.

Crash Landing, the Stevan Dohanos painting that illustrated Caterpillar advertisements of April 1944.

132

Engineers of the 2nd Infantry Division constructing a bypass for heavy equipment to cross the Han River, in order to give support to the infantry. September 25, 1950.

Two Army corporals move their bulldozer aside to let traffic pass, as men of the 3rd Engineer Battalion 24th Infantry Division repair a road near the front lines in Korea. March 7, 1951.

A U.S. Army private bulldozer operator for the 630 Engineer Light Equipment Company bulldozes crushed rock from a rock crushing machine. February 23, 1951.

Caterpillar D7 and Caterpillar grader somewhere in Korea.

A Caterpillar Diesel No. 12 Motor Grader and D7 extending the runway at Ebee Field, Fort Belvoir, Virginia. October 1950.

140

Caterpillar equipment off-loaded from a U.S. Air Force C-124 Douglas Globemaster.

CATERPILLAR TRACTORS IN WORLD WAR I
Built by Holt Manufacturing Company

	18 H.P.	45 H.P.	55 H.P.	60 H.P.	75 H.P.	120 H.P.	TOTAL
United States Government	2	74	2102	0	370	433	2081
British War Department	1	1	1	43	1362	243	1051
French War Department	0	352	0	0	18	0	370
Russian Government	0	0	0	20	60	0	80
Total	**3**	**407**	**2103**	**63**	**1810**	**676**	**5082**

Built for the U.S. Government by Other Manufacturers under Holt Patent License and Holt Supervision

Reo Motor Car Company	5 Ton Tractors	1477
Maxwell Motor Car Company	6 Ton Tractors (Renault Tanks)	225
	5 Ton Tractors	2193
Federal Motor Truck Company	2 1/2 Ton Tractors	87
Interstate Motor Company	2 1/2 Ton Tractors	7
Chandler Motor Car Company	10 Ton Tractors	700
Total		**4689**

The Iconografix Photo Archive Series includes:

JOHN DEERE MODEL D Photo Archive	ISBN 1-882256-00-X
JOHN DEERE MODEL A Photo Archive	ISBN 1-882256-12-3
JOHN DEERE MODEL B Photo Archive	ISBN 1-882256-01-8
JOHN DEERE 30 SERIES Photo Archive	ISBN 1-882256-13-1
FARMALL REGULAR Photo Archive	ISBN 1-882256-14-X
FARMALL F-SERIES Photo Archive	ISBN 1-882256-02-6
FARMALL MODEL H Photo Archive	ISBN 1-882256-03-4
FARMALL MODEL M Photo Archive	ISBN 1-882256-15-8
CATERPILLAR THIRTY Photo Archive	ISBN 1-882256-04-2
CATERPILLAR SIXTY Photo Archive	ISBN 1-882256-05-0
TWIN CITY TRACTOR Photo Archive	ISBN 1-882256-06-9
MINNEAPOLIS-MOLINE U-SERIES Photo Archive	ISBN 1-882256-07-7
HART-PARR Photo Archive	ISBN 1-882256-08-5
OLIVER TRACTOR Photo Archive	ISBN 1-882256-09-3
HOLT TRACTORS Photo Archive	ISBN 1-882256-10-7
RUSSELL GRADERS Photo Archive	ISBN 1-882256-11-5
MACK MODEL AB Photo Archive	ISBN 1-882256-18-2
MACK MODEL B, 1953-66 Photo Archive	ISBN 1-882256-19-0
CATERPILLAR MILITARY TRACTORS VOLUME 1 Photo Archive	ISBN 1-882256-16-6
CATERPILLAR MILITARY TRACTORS VOLUME 2 Photo Archive	ISBN 1-882256-17-4
LE MANS 1950: THE BRIGGS CUNNINGHAM CAMPAIGN Photo Archive	ISBN 1-882256-21-2
SEBRING 12-HOUR RACE 1970 Photo Archive	ISBN 1-882256-20-4
IMPERIAL 1955-1963 Photo Archive	ISBN 1-882256-22-0

The Iconografix Photo Archive Series is available from direct mail specialty book dealers and bookstores throughout the world, or can be ordered from the publisher.

For information write to:

Iconografix
P.O. Box 609
Osceola, Wisconsin 54020 USA

Telephone: (715) 294-2792
(800) 289-3504 (USA and Canada)
Fax: (715) 294-3414